Christian BAYA DIAKILEKE

Artificial Intelligence and Expert Systems course

Christian BAYA DIAKILEKE

Artificial Intelligence and Expert Systems course

ScienciaScripts

Imprint
Any brand names and product names mentioned in this book are subject to trademark, brand or patent protection and are trademarks or registered trademarks of their respective holders. The use of brand names, product names, common names, trade names, product descriptions etc. even without a particular marking in this work is in no way to be construed to mean that such names may be regarded as unrestricted in respect of trademark and brand protection legislation and could thus be used by anyone.

Cover image: www.ingimage.com

This book is a translation from the original published under ISBN 978-620-6-72047-8.

Publisher:
Sciencia Scripts
is a trademark of
Dodo Books Indian Ocean Ltd. and OmniScriptum S.R.L publishing group

120 High Road, East Finchley, London, N2 9ED, United Kingdom
Str. Armeneasca 28/1, office 1, Chisinau MD-2012, Republic of Moldova, Europe
Managing Directors: Ieva Konstantinova, Victoria Ursu
info@omniscriptum.com

Printed at: see last page
ISBN: 978-620-8-53176-8

GENERAL OBJECTIVES

At the end of this course, the student of the **Third Degree (L3 LMD) in Computer Management** should be able to:

- ✓ **Analyze texts**: whether spoken or written, artificial intelligence is becoming increasingly adept at understanding and using language to respond automatically to a variety of requests. Today, it is used, for example, to manage customer relations, on the Internet or by telephone. Conversational agents, or *chatbots*, are intelligent systems that can maintain a conversation in natural language. They are based on different technological building blocks: text recognition, speech recognition, facial expression recognition...

- ✓ **Modeling knowledge to help make decisions**: artificial intelligence enables us to encode a body of knowledge, reproduce standard reasoning and use this information to make decisions. For example, it is now possible to use multiple, complex data to help doctors propose personalized treatments for prostate cancer.

- ✓ **Generate knowledge through *machine* learning**: thanks to artificial intelligence, the machine becomes capable of spotting trends or correlations in a very large volume of data, adapting its analyses and behaviors and thus creating its own knowledge based on accumulated experience. This makes it possible to offer highly refined predictions on energy consumption, or the evolution of the behavior of a machine or a building. The predictive rules derived from this are merely the result of what has already taken place; they are not general laws.

- ✓ **Analyze images or scenes in real time**: recognize manufacturing defects or detect faces. For example, some factories have robots that detect technical problems and defects in real time, and correct or stop production. To analyze large quantities of visual data simultaneously, researchers are developing software based on deep neural networks, which enable computers to acquire *deep* learning capabilities.

- ✓ **Perform actions**: for example, artificial intelligence can imitate and reproduce to perfection certain human gestures, such as administering a vaccine using a robotic hand.

CONTENTS

INTRODUCTION GENERAL

Today, with a simple phrase, we can find out the weather, set an alarm, be notified of appointments, with directions to get there and increasingly precise results over time... This is the emerging face AI in our daily lives. But beyond these practical but somewhat anecdotal uses, artificial intelligence covers a vast field, with existing or potential applications that are almost infinite.

Translation , image recognition , facial recognition, voice assistants , chatbots, autonomous vehicles, agriculture, banking, optimizing sales prospecting, predictive maintenance, medical diagnostic assistance, facility management and smart buildings, improving recruitment processes, reducing energy consumption... Artificial intelligence is a science that is disrupting every sector, every field.

To better understand this course, the following notions are practically indispensable for finding your way around the complex world of intelligent machines:

1. Algorithm

A set of instructions given to a machine or computer program to methodically solve a problem. The algorithm executes repetitive processes, broken down into steps or tasks. An adaptive algorithm is capable of modifying its responses or the data it processes according to changes in its environment.

2. Bot

Software that automatically performs a specific task. To be distinguished from a robot, which assumes a "physical" envelope, with mechanical constraints and which, in the collective imagination, has a humanoid shape.

3. Chatbot cobot

A chatbot is a conversational bot (from the English chat: to chat), i.e. a software program, capable of understanding questions formulated by a user and providing answers in natural language, either written or spoken. A cobot is a collaborative bot, and sometimes a robot, that assists a human colleague in a specific task .

4. Deep learning

Branch of machine learning based on artificial neural networks. Deep learning uses probability calculus to analyze and categorize from very large masses of data. This approach is "connectionist" as opposed to the "symbolic" approach of expert systems (see below). Deep learning is at the root of the meteoric progress made by AI in recent years in speech and image recognition. On the other hand, the use of probabilities in data analysis does not provide a 100% "explanation" of the choices made by the machine.

5. Weak AI/ Strong AI

Weak AI refers to a machine capable of solving problems in a specific domain, such as chess or cooking, to the exclusion of others. Strong AI, also known as "generalist" AI, is capable of adapting to any environment, suggesting artificial "consciousness" and even intentionality in its choice of options. This is the stuff of science fiction for most experts... but not all!

6. Machine learning

Computer science discipline that brings together machine learning techniques based on various types of data (text, images, sounds, etc.). Using mathematical and statistical methods, the machine correlates the data provided to establish rules for classification, perception and prediction. For example, to distinguish between a road sign and a pedestrian.

7. Operational research

This discipline of mathematics explores how to determine the best decision when faced with a complex problem. For example, choosing the shortest route between two points, with budget constraints and shifting congestion. AI is fond of this type of mathematical method and model.

8. Neural network

Succession of mathematical or statistical micro-calculations that "feed one another, like a network of biological neurons in the human brain. When equipped with a sufficient base of examples and "coached" by learning algorithm, these neural networks are able to compare and reconcile a new case with another in their database. For example, to recognize a dog in a hairball with legs.

9. Expert system (or rule-based system)

This software gives recommendations based on rules provided by human experts: business procedures, regulations, standards, etc. This AI is called symbolic, because it works according to formal principles and reasoning. It can, for example, calculate insurance premiums or point out an anomaly in a train or plane timetable.

CHAPTER I. BASIC CONCEPTS

I.1. Definitions

What does the term "artificial intelligence" mean? Definitions are available in scientific literature and specialized and non-specialized dictionaries. How does an AI program differ from others? We'll try to answer both these questions. First, let's look at the definitions provided by dictionaries. The *Petit Robert* dictionary offers one:

"A.I., part of computer science whose purpose is to simulate cognitive faculties in order to supplement the human being in performing functions that are agreed, in a given context, to require intelligence."

In this way, the system does not produce an intelligent action, but merely simulates it. If the machine can perform an operation that requires human intelligence, it can be considered intelligent.

The encyclopedic dictionary by Bernard LAMIZET and Amhed SILEM continues the comparison by adding the notion competition between man and machine. These authors see artificial intelligence as the future of computing.

"Discipline whose aim is the study and design of systems whose behavior approaches what we call human intelligence. Because of the ambition of this field and the number of areas into which it has split over the years, it is a major component of computer science. What's more, it is undoubtedly the field with the widest prospects, since it is a competitor to the human mind, whose unfathomable secrets we are still a long way from unlocking.

Raoul SMITH introduces the notion of learning from environment and experience, and introduces the concept of symbolic representation of knowledge.

This enables inferences to be made, i.e. reasoning based on the formalized knowledge produced. It also highlights the thorny problem of understanding natural or human language, one of the challenges of future artificial intelligence. It's easy to see that the term covers a vast field of research.

Popular articles and books also provide definitions. Jean-François DORTIER introduces notions of analysis, problem-solving, decision-making, learning and perception. Artificial intelligence has developed these techniques over the last fifty years.

"Field of computer science that focuses on building intelligent programs, i.e. programs that can analyze an environment, solve problems, make decisions, learn, perceive."

Alain BONNET highlights two AI objectives: to understand the nature of intelligence (a goal shared by the cognitive sciences) and to simulate intelligence:

"Artificial intelligence is a discipline that aims to understand the nature of intelligence by building computer programs that mimic human intelligence."

"Artificial intelligence is concerned with the cognitive processes used by human beings to perform intelligent tasks.

This does not mean, however, that the computer actually produces intelligent driving. It is the observation of human behavior requiring a degree of intelligence that enables modeling and execution on the machine.

Jacques FERBER, professor of computer science and specialist in distributed artificial intelligence, emphasizes the comparison between the performance of human intelligence and that of the machine. We're not talking about a general form of intelligence, but a multifactorial one.

"The term "artificial intelligence" has been used to designate a research project consisting of designing an intelligent machine, i.e. one capable of succeeding as well as a human being in tasks deemed complex."

The AI method consists of elucidating certain brain activities and reproducing them on a computer. Understanding, communicating, problem-solving, strategizing and decision-making are all part of this set. Artificial intelligence takes its inspiration from the study of these behaviors in humans and proposes a computer model. It goes hand in hand with the development of cognitive sciences.

How does artificial intelligence differ from traditional programming? Its aim is to understand the nature of intelligence and to build programs that simulate the behaviors associated with this quality.

At the outset, the computer scientist seeks to solve a problem. The program must therefore use a set of mechanisms to find a method likely to provide a solution. Artificial intelligence thus differs essentially from conventional programming. In the case of conventional programming, it is the human who constructs the reasoning to be applied, and the program is executed until the predictable results are achieved. In other words, programming is deterministic. In contrast, in an AI application, "*it's the program that chooses the path to follow*. The path is not predetermined.

Thus, the research method in artificial intelligence consists of starting with a human activity deemed intelligent (or intelligent task), hypothesizing about the processes involved in performing the task in question, incorporating them into a program, observing the behavior and results produced by the program, refining the initial theory and modifying the program.

First of all, the main characteristic of a program is its use of a symbolic representation of the aspect of the world concerned. Artificial intelligence uses high-level programming languages, or declarative languages, which enable us to manipulate symbols that structure our knowledge. This representation establishes a relationship between the real world in which the problem to be addressed is situated and the symbolic system used to solve it, which is not necessarily numerical.

Artificial intelligence separates the knowledge to be processed by the program and the modes of reasoning or inference (deductive or inductive) likely to manipulate this knowledge and provide a solution to the problem posed. Secondly, the use of heuristics is another fundamental characteristic.

These can be defined as "*an informal method with no guarantee of success*". "*A heuristic approach consists, when faced with a problem, of trying one path while keeping open the possibility of trying others if the one that seemed promising did not quickly lead to a solution.*"

The program is faced with a number of difficulties. It must be able to provide a solution to the problem posed, despite absence of all the data relating to the problem. It must also be able to cope with contradictory or conflicting inputs. It must be able to learn.

Alain BONNET defines learning in computing as "*the ability to improve one's performance by taking into account past mistakes*. This process involves the ability to generalize, to discover analogies, to choose omissions, i.e. to forget unnecessary details.

The main characteristics presented above show the difference between classical programming, which is procedural and deterministic, and the methods used in artificial intelligence. But what is AI used for? Let's take a look at the fields of application of artificial intelligence research.

I.2. AI field

The field of artificial intelligence seeks to understand how humans think, and strives to build intelligent entities.

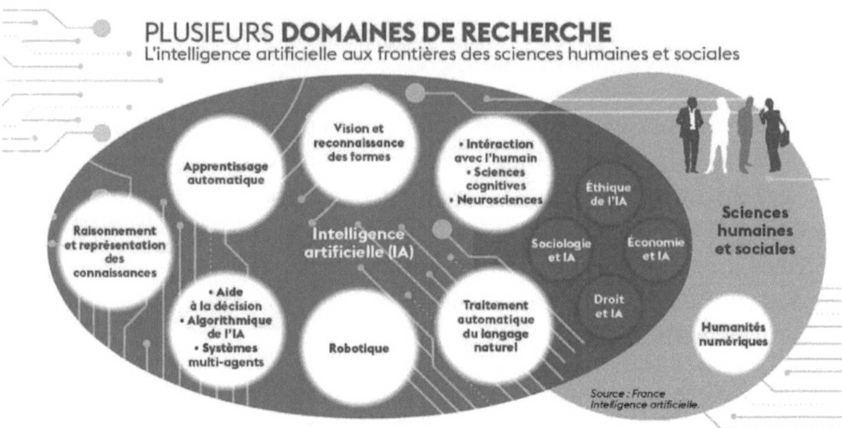

AI research covers a wide range of fields. These include

- **Knowledge representation**: if software is to be able to manipulate knowledge, it needs to be able to represent it symbolically. This is one of the most important areas of artificial intelligence research.

- **Natural language processing**: whether it's a question of translating a text into another language or summarizing it, the crucial problem to be solved is that of understanding it. Software can be said to understand a text when it can represent it in a form independent of the language in which it written: this is a very difficult task, but significant progress has already been made.

- **Problem solving**. Games provide a good illustration of this field: the world champion in backgammon has been a program for some years now, and this will probably also be the case for chess in the near future. The game of Go is much more resistant to the efforts of game programmers.

- **Speech recognition**: progress is much slower than imagined, but constant. We are still a long way from being able to produce software capable of recognizing the words of any speaker, essentially because understanding a word or a sentence requires great deal of extra-language information, such as context and knowledge of the world in which we live.

- **Handwriting recognition**: even typewriting recognition is not an easy problem, although there are some very powerful software packages on the market. Handwriting, on the other hand, poses even more difficult problems, as it can pose unsolvable problems for us too.

- **Face recognition**: long considered to be one of the most difficult problems in artificial intelligence, neural networks have produced some interesting results.

- **Robotics**

Research robots: Rodney Brooks' COG robot from MIT in 1991 is able to see, hear and reflect, and in particular to look at itself in a mirror by identifying with its image. COG reacts to its visuals as a child would. It is the most advanced robot of its generation.

Exhibition robots. In 2000 Honda presented Asimo (Advanced Step in Innovative Mobility), an exhibition robot representing the culmination of 14 years of research. It was designed under the direction of engineer Masato Hirose. This little android measures 1.20 m and weighs 53 kg. It moves at 16km/h but is capable of running at a moderate pace (12km/h), hopping, dancing and climbing up and down stairs. During a public performance, Asimo misses a step and is alert, showing signs of intelligence and then falling and being unable to recover, revealing all the powerlessness of men to breathe life and fundamental reflexes into him. Both fascinating and pathetic, his fall down the stairs revealed just how far we still have to go to create a fully autonomous android.

- **Learning**: It was understood very early on that software would have to have autonomous learning capabilities to be truly qualified as intelligence.

- **Medical diagnostic assistance**: Diagnostic assistance software has been designed to provide medical practitioners with innovative, easy-to-use diagnostic tools. They are primarily based on patients' medical records, and are published by medical specialty.

- **Expert systems**: an expert system is software capable of simulating the behavior of a human expert performing a specific task. The success of artificial intelligence in this field is undeniable, due to the target nature of the activity it is asked to simulate. Expert systems have also played an important role in the evolution of artificial intelligence. Indeed, this branch has enjoyed a certain success since the 1980s.

Chapter 3 of this course will focus on the Expert System, taking into account the practical work scheduled.

The aim of these systems is to model human expertise in a specific domain. They comprise two modules: a knowledge base and an inference engine. They are, in FERBER's words, "*computer programs capable of replacing human beings in their most complex tasks, which require experience, know-how and a certain form of reasoning*".

I.3. Practical applications AI

Artificial intelligence techniques and methods are used in a multitude of fields. Here are just a few practical applications: expert systems in medicine, banking and finance; computer network management and control systems; ticket reservation systems; systems used in air transport management; *datamining* systems and *datawarehousing*; software agents, search engines, Internet software (for on-line purchasing). Defense systems, too, have been quick to integrate AI technology. In fact, military budgets have often financed AI research.

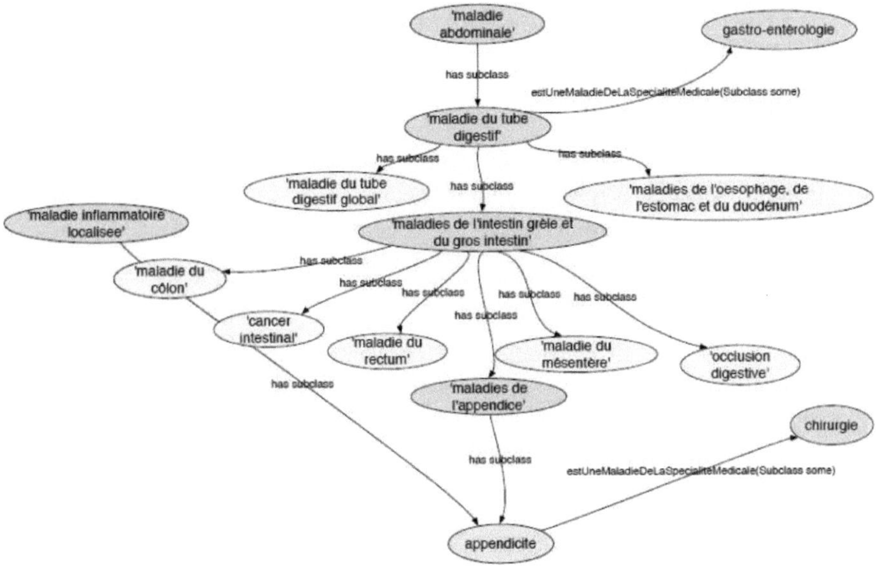

This discipline has led to the development of methods and algorithms capable facilitating the operations required network maintenance and document retrieval, among many other activities.

CHAPTER II. MULTI-AGENT SYSTEMS AND THEIR INTERACTIONS

II.1. Definitions

In **computer science**, a multi-agent system (MAS) is a system made up of a set of agents (a process, a robot, a human being, an ant, etc.), active in a certain environment and interacting according to certain rules. An agent is an entity characterized by the fact it is at least partially autonomous, which rules out centralized control of the overall system.

A focus of research in distributed artificial intelligence, multi-agent systems constitute a interesting possibility of modeling human and animal societies, and as such have a wide range of applications, including the human sciences.

II.2. Origin and technical aspects

II.2.1. Origin

One of the great sources of inspiration for multi-agent systems has been the study of the social behavior of certain insect families. In this field, please refer to the articles on Collective Intelligence and Distributed Intelligence.

ADMs can be seen as the meeting of various domains:

- ✓ Artificial intelligence for the agent's decision-making aspects
- ✓ Distributed artificial intelligence distributed execution
- ✓ Distributed systems for interaction
- ✓ Software *agent* approach and evolution to increasingly autonomous software components
- ✓ Communicating objects

An example: the video game metaphor

An ADMM can be represented by one of the virtual communities increasingly found in today's video games. Let's take the example of a game that simulates the life of a family. The SMA can be broken down into several dimensions. First, an environment with a metric.

We can think of it as the house and garden where our little family lives. Next, the SMA can have a set of passive objects on which our agents can intervene. These include all the objects in the house, as well as food.

An ADM is made up of agents. These agents are active and autonomous, interacting with their environment, objects and other agents. These agents are identified as family members. Next, we add a set of relationships between objects and agents, which defines an organization. We can, for example, express family links different individuals, but also deal with notions of property (which object belongs to whom?).

Finally, we integrate a set of operators that enable agents to act on objects or other agents (the son can eat a yogurt, walk his dog or talk to his sister), and sensors that enable agents to learn about changes in the environment and other agents (the yogurt fell on the floor, Dad asked me to take the dog out). This is what we call an ADM. In computer science, an agent is an autonomous program possessing a body of knowledge and acting according to its own rules.

The five challenges of ADM

Five main issues can be identified when creating multi-agent systems:

First, the problem of **action**: how can a set of agents act simultaneously in a shared environment, and how does this environment interact in return with the agents? Underlying issues include agent representation of the environment, collaboration between agents, and multi-agent planning.

Next, the issue of **the agent and its relationship to the world**, which is represented by the cognitive model available to the agent. The individual in a multi-agent society must be capable of implementing the actions that best meet his or her objectives. This decision-making ability is linked to a "mental state" that reflects the agent's perceptions, representations, beliefs and a certain number of "psychic" parameters (desires, tendencies, etc.). The issue of the individual and his relationship to the world also covers the notion of the agent's commitment to a third-party agent.

Multi-agent systems also involve **studying the nature of interactions**, as a source of possibilities on the one hand and constraints on the other. Interaction issues concern the means of interaction (what language? what support?), and the analysis and design of forms of interaction between agents. The notions of collaboration and cooperation (taking cooperation to mean collaboration + coordination of actions + conflict resolution) are central here.

Then there's the question **of adaptation**, in terms of individual adaptation or learning the one hand, and collective adaptation or evolution on the other.

Finally, there remains the question of **the actual realization and implementation of ADMs**, by structuring programming languages into several types ranging from the L5 type language, or formalization and specification language, to the L1 type language, which is the actual implementation language. Between the two, we find the language of communication between agents, description of environmental laws and knowledge representation.

II.2.2. Multi-agent system architecture

Taking up the five previous issues, we can describe some elements of the architecture of a multi-agent system.

Agents need to be equipped with multiple decision and planning systems. Decision theories are a field of study in their own right. In the category of interactions with the environment, another recurrent problem of agent systems is that of pathfinding (with its best-known algorithm, the A* algorithm).[1]

[1] **In computer science, more specifically in artificial intelligence, the A* search algorithm (pronounced A *star*) is an algorithm for finding a path in a graph between a given initial node and a given final node. Because of its simplicity, it is often presented as a typical example of a planning , a algorithmfield of artificial intelligence. The A* algorithm was created so that the first solution found would be one of the best, which is why it is famous in applications such as video games, where speed of calculation is more important than accuracy of results. This algorithm was first proposed by Peter E. Hart, Nils John Nilsson and Bertram Raphael in 1968.**

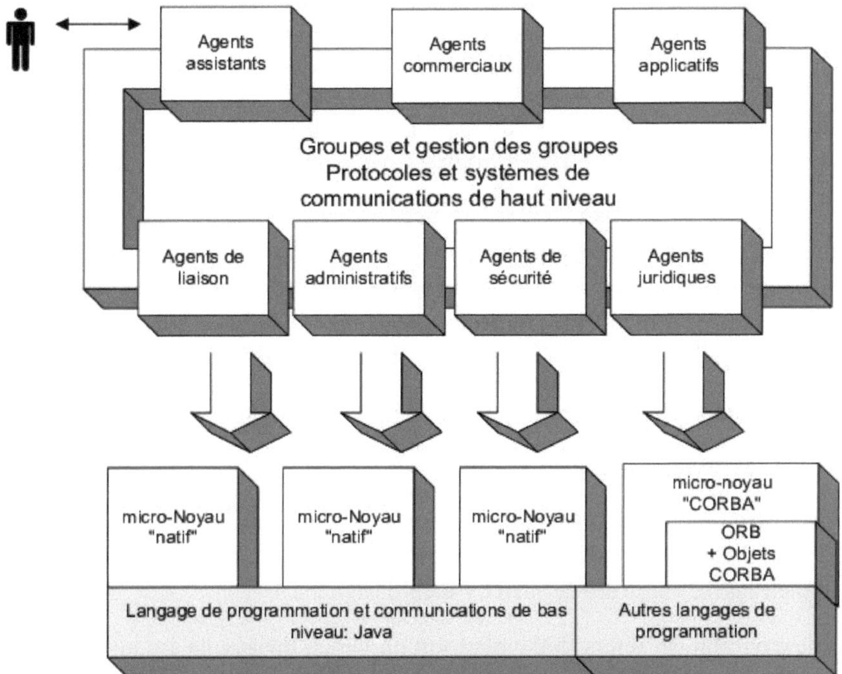

The architecture of a multi-agent system running on a network.

Pathfinding : The search of path, commonly referred to as ***pathfinding***, is an intelligence artificial problem that relates more generally to the field of planning and solution finding. It consists in finding a way to move in an environment between a starting point and an end point, taking into account various constraints.

Agents must have a cognitive model: Here too, several models exist, one of the most classic being the BDI model (*Beliefs-Desires-Intentions*). It considers, on the one hand, the agent's set of beliefs (*Beliefs*) about its environment, which are the result of its knowledge and perceptions, and, on the other hand, a set of objectives (*Desires*). By crossing these two sets, we obtain a new set of intentions (*Intentions*), which can then be directly translated into actions.

The agents must be equipped with a communication system. Several specialized languages have been developed for this purpose: *Knowledge*

Query and Manipulation Language (KQML), and more recently, the FIPA-ACL standard (ACL for *Agent Communication Language*) created by the *Foundation for Intelligent Physical Agents* FIPA. The latter standard is based in particular on John Searle's theory of speech acts.

The issue of adaptation is a thorny one, and the subject of much research. We could, however, cite the example certain viruses, both biological and computer-related, capable of adapting to their environment by mutating.

Finally, the actual implementation of the multi-agent system, while not strictly speaking part of the system architecture, is worth mentioning through the example of the many programming languages that have been developed for artificial intelligence research purposes. These include **Prolog** and **LISP**.

These architectural elements apply to a system made up of cognitive agents.

II.3. Classifying intelligent agents

There are several ways of classifying agents. They can be grouped according to environment, the PUSH/PULL or CLIENT/SERVICE dichotomy, or according to their tasks. These are defined by their designers.

The environment refers to the platform on which the agents are installed. There are three main classes of intelligent agents: PC agents, Internet agents and intranet agents. *Desktop agents* are embedded in the computer's operating system (Windows, Mac OS, etc.). They are known as assistants. Their function is to help the user perform an automated task, such as installing new software or a new *plug-and-play* peripheral.

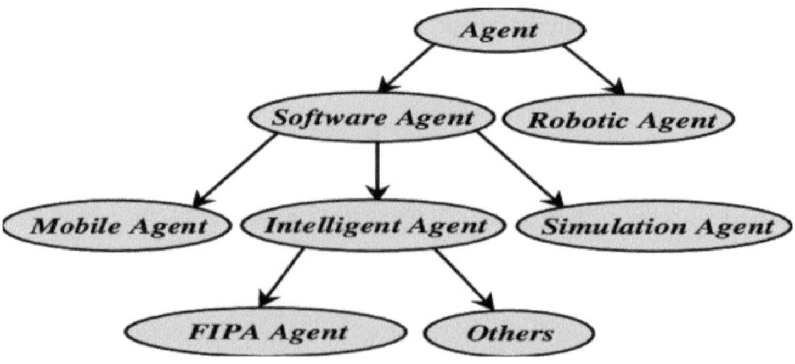

Intranet agents retrieve resources from company servers. Internet agents help users search for documents on the Internet. Engines and meta-engines fall into this category.

A second distinction is between PULL and PUSH agents. The English verb *pull* means to pull towards oneself, while the word *push* means to send to someone else. The user initiates the query by setting up an agent based on keywords or more complex expressions. He delegates the task to a PULL agent such as an engine or meta-engine. However, the user interacts with the program by transforming the query according to the results returned.

With PUSH technology, on the other hand, the user is passive. PUSH-type software enables access to thematic or topical information channels, such as TV or newspaper channels. Information is sent regularly to subscribers according their pre-defined profile or interests, or learned through the vigilance of the computer program. PointCast, Marimba and BlackWeb are examples of PUSH software. Google (*news alerts*) and certain meta-engines such as Copernic have integrated this type of activity.

Selective delivery agents are part of PUSH technology. Their aim is to find information of interest to users, without them having to request it. The system works as follows. The user signs a contract with information provider, who sends him a selection of documents based on his tastes and interests. An intelligent agent automatically selects the documents and establishes a link between the agent installed on the user's computer and that of the provider's server. American newspapers such as *The New York Times* offer this type of service.

Alert and watch agents monitor an information source or theme to alert the user according to a predefined query. They send e-mail messages when content changes. This type of agent includes Url-Minder and Net Mind High lighter.

The last classification describes the uses intended by software publishers: the tasks performed by the agent. Let's take a look at these various types program, noting that this list is by no means exhaustive.

A filtering agent is designed to examine incoming mail and destroy unwanted e-mails in the mailbox, eliminate irrelevant information from a query, and search for and prepare information from a variety of sources. (Some examples: News Hound, ZDNet personal View or NewsPage Direct).

A *retrieval* agent downloads an entire site to the hard disk, facilitating offline content analysis. Off-line *notifiers* alert the user when a site changes, when important information arrives or when an important event occurs.

Search agents identify relevant information on the Internet in relation to a set of engines and according to user preferences. They can incorporate a learning module. What we call an agent here is the subject of a set of functionalities introduced in intelligent agent software packages of the meta-engine type.

We also come across off-line *delivery agents* who, as their name suggests, send personalized information to users on their hard disk. The connection is not established while the received documents are being read or consulted, which used to reduce bandwidth consumption.

PUSH technology has emerged as a solution to the problems posed by the exponential growth of documents on the Web. It's extremely difficult and costly (in terms of time) to find the information you're looking for using PULL alone. PUSH, on the other hand, enables web users to receive documents prepared for downloading:

"The solution was devised by PointCast. It's about gathering the information that users are looking for, mixing it with advertising and announcements and sending it to them while they're sleeping!... With push, it's the information that finds the user. With push, it's the information that finds the user.

However, PUSH does have its drawbacks: the amount of information sent to and stored on the hard disk can be considerable and quickly become difficult to manage, hence the need for high-performance internal search engines.

The client/server dichotomy also enables classification. Some agents can be downloaded and installed on the user's hard disk. Others, on the other hand, operate from the agent owner's server, in client-server mode.

The web user logs in and uses the services of the technology provided free of charge. The advantage of client-side agents lies in their greater parameterization than agents located on a remote server. The last classification mode describes the uses intended by software publishers: the tasks performed by the agent.

Shopping *agents* make it easier to find the best price for a given product. They are not necessarily appreciated by the owners of retail websites, and their entry into a site may be prohibited. Pure and perfect competition on the Internet is not universally accepted. This type of technology is gradually being integrated into search engine and portal sites.

Chat agents (*chatterbots*) are proving capable of conversing with a user.

The first of its kind, Eliza, acted like a psychoanalyst asking her patient questions to get her talking. Since then, *chatterbots* have been designed to introduce a form of dialogue and interactivity to certain commercial websites. The bot can answer questions posed by the Internet user about a product or service, or send data sheets based on keywords identified in the visitor's statement.

Classified agents examine product offers in databases according to the subject or field specified by the Internet user. They send the results by e-mail. *Announcement* agents remind users of important events or appointments. This type of agent can be installed online or on a PC hard disk.

Other types exist, some specialized in books (*book agents*), who search for new publications according to user preferences. *Business information monitoring agents* filter business news, publications and reports posted on the Internet by companies. *Financial service* agents provide financial information based on the user's personal portfolio. Finally, *job agents* search for potential job candidates based on CVs posted online.

A pattern of use emerges from all these descriptions: the user delegates a specific task and receives the results of the operation automatically, without having to repeat the request.

Most of these agents were invented in response to economic demand. They correspond to consumer or business needs anticipated by software developers and publishers.

Some are offered as freeware, and the cost of development is borne by financing methods such as partnerships with commercial sites, advertising, but often on a subscription basis for the time being. These agents can easily be integrated into global information retrieval systems such as portals. What's more, computer users can build their own agents using the "api" (*application programming interface*) offered by the latter.

So how do you simply define an intelligent agent? It's a program that performs a task on the user's initiative. It is autonomous and can automate its tasks. It acts by delegation.

The term most often designates an information retrieval program, if we examine the definitions on the web. Here are a few definitions given by Google (*code definir: intelligent agent*) confirming our point:

· In computing, an agent is the equivalent of a software robot. It is a program that carries out tasks in the manner of an automaton, according to the instructions given by its author(f) .[2]

· [3]Software element (program) capable of executing certain tasks on a permanent basis (network monitoring, documentary research, etc.) which only manifests itself when needed (request for intervention, end of research, etc.). ...

· [4]Software designed to facilitate the retrieval and management of information on the Internet. It has its own attributes and acts to perform a number of tasks for another software agent or a human ...

· (n.) Object of a server that executes various requests (HTTP, NNTP, SMTP and FTP) on behalf of the user. In a way, the intelligent agent acts as a client for the server, making requests filled in by the[5] server.

---

[2] http://www. wikipedia.org/wiki/Agent_intelligent

[3] http://www. revuesim.free.fr/index.php

[4] http://www. aeris.11vm serv.net/cours/util_outils/glos.html

[5] http://www. docs.sun.com/app/docs/doc/819-4628/6n6p2pm93

CHAPTER III. BASIC CONCEPTS OF EXPERT SYSTEMS

III.1. What is an Expert System?

Expert Systems (ES) are computer systems equipped to behave like human experts. They must possess the skills of human experts in a specific field, and make use of them when called upon. What makes a system a system expert? We'll answer this question by presenting the birth, history and general architecture of these SEs in general.

III.2. A little history:

The DENDRAL program began in the late 60s at Stanford University under the direction of B. Buchanan, with E. Feigenbaun and Nobel Prize winner J. Leberg. Leberg. This program determines the structure of a molecule from the mass spectrum established by a mass spectogram.

The forms that a molecular compound can take were introduced by Leberg, are numerous and subject to constant enrichment as new compounds appear. This is why, building on the ideas of Newell and Simon and young Stanford researchers (D. waterman among others), E. Feigenbaum had the idea of separating Ledeberg's reasoning and knowledge from the rest of the computer machinery: the first expert system was born. We recognize in it the particular architecture of knowledge-based systems. It was the first program which a non-computer scientist, the first "expert", contributed his or her knowledge, identified and valued as such.

The success of DENDRAL was to lead, in the 1975-80s, to expert systems. The first and best-known system of this era was MYCIN, designed at Stanford University by Shortliffe. It is an expert system for medical diagnosis. It was the first to take uncertain knowledge into account. It will soon be followed by PROSPECTOR (Duda and Hart, Nilsson and a whole team at SRI). The success of MYCIN, which works as well as the experts, when the experts agree, and the media success of PROSPECTOR, were to lead to a certain craze.

The different parts an expert system:

The heart of an AI system is made up of three parts:

1. **A knowledge base** in which **all the knowledge** required to solve a given problem **in a given field** is stored in an appropriate form .
2. **An operating mechanism (inference engine),** which is a set of programs capable of **translating human reasoning** (heuristics, forward and backward

progression, decomposition into subsets, etc.). These programs use the knowledge stored in the knowledge base to solve the problem posed by the user, giving starting hypotheses.

3. **A database of the facts** of the problem to be solved, which is in fact a working memory in which the **initial hypotheses** will be stored, to which **new facts** will added as the operating mechanism progresses.

In A.I., a system must have two other parts, which are in fact interface modules with the outside world:

4. **A module for interaction with potential users**: this dialogue interface must be as user-friendly as possible. This module is linked to the operating mechanism.

5. **A knowledge-acquisition support module**, which is above all a dialogue interface between the knowledge base and the domain experts who need to feed it.

Generally speaking, an expert system is a tool capable reproducing the cognitive mechanisms of an expert in a particular field. This is one of the paths leading to artificial intelligence.

More precisely, an expert system **is software** capable of answering questions by reasoning on the basis of known facts and rules. In particular, it can be used as a decision-making tool.

An expert system consists of 3 parts:

✓ **A fact base (knowledge base)** is a collection of knowledge (provided by a human expert) represented by rules,

✓ **A rule base (knowledge domain)** is the specialist's body of knowledge that enables him or her to solve specific problems.

✓ **An inference engine (inference mechanism)** is a mechanism that enables the expert system to reason and draw conclusions.

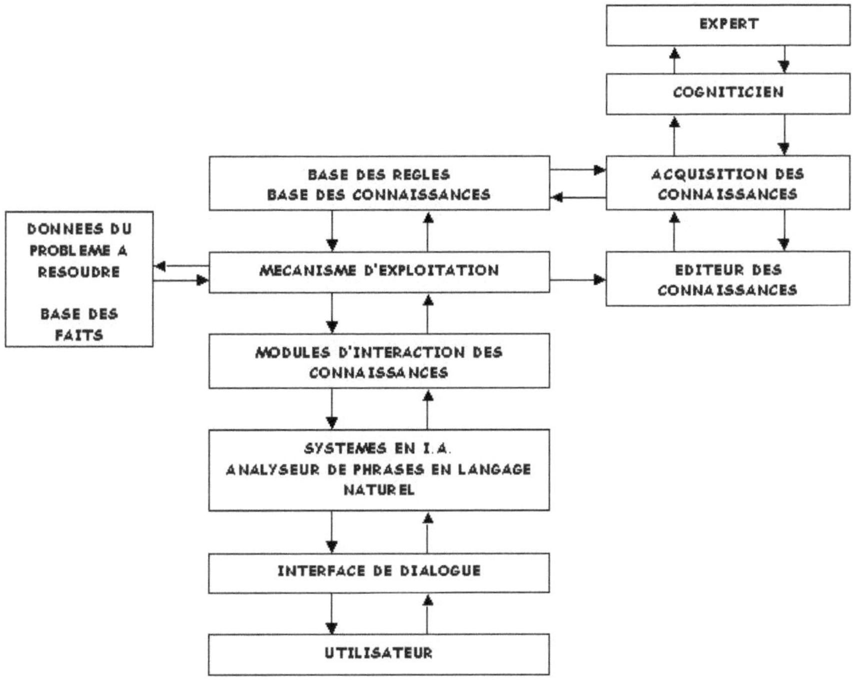

ARCHITECTURE GENERALE D'UN SYSTEME EXPERT

A knowledge base is completely **independent of the knowledge exploitation mechanism**. The expert can add, modify or delete knowledge without having to worry about the operating mechanism.

The knowledge base operating :

The knowledge base will exploit the fact base to find the solution(s) (otherwise it will fail). The system attempts to **simulate human reasoning** using certain concepts:

- Heuristics (as opposed to algorithms).
- Breaking down a problem into sub-problems.
- Forward and progression.
- Evolution towards the solution through a progression different successive steps.

Reasoning can be certain: knowledge is weighted.

Reasoning can be uncertain: a plausibility (or likelihood) coefficient is attached to each piece of knowledge, making it possible to use fuzzy or uncertain logic, in which there is a continuum of possibilities ranging from true to false (or from zero to one).

Knowledge base: set of knowledge (provided by a human expert) represented by rules

Types of knowledge

Explicit knowledge: what I can express

Explicit knowledge [Smith, 2001; Dienes et al., 1991] is the body of knowledge that an individual can consciously memorize and retrieve, and then express through language. It is often learned in verbal form. They are associated with explicit memory (figure A), which concerns all biographical events (episodic memory) and the memory of concepts and objects (semantic memory) [Squire, 1992; Squire and Zola, 1996].

This knowledge, which can be formalized and transmitted, can be expressed by the individual and can therefore be stored in an external format (document, reports, etc.). It is considered easily extractable [Nonaka and Takeuchi, 1995], since it can be easily verbalized.

Implicit knowledge: what I know how to do

Implicit knowledge is non-expressible knowledge of which the individual is unaware [Schacter, 1987]. It is linked to implicit memory. The learning of such knowledge is implicit: it is through imitation, practice, life and experience that an individual acquires this type of knowledge. They include procedural knowledge (linked, for example, to motor skills such as riding a bike), perceptual memory (memory for shapes, colors, smells and sounds), reflexes and non-associative learning such as habituation and sensitization [Squire, 1992; Squire and Zola, 1996]. This knowledge is important because it is associated with a person's experience and has a direct impact on reasoning. Dienes and Berry [1997] present implicit knowledge as inflexible, inaccessible and linked to the nature of the information (i.e. the characteristics of the material) used during learning.

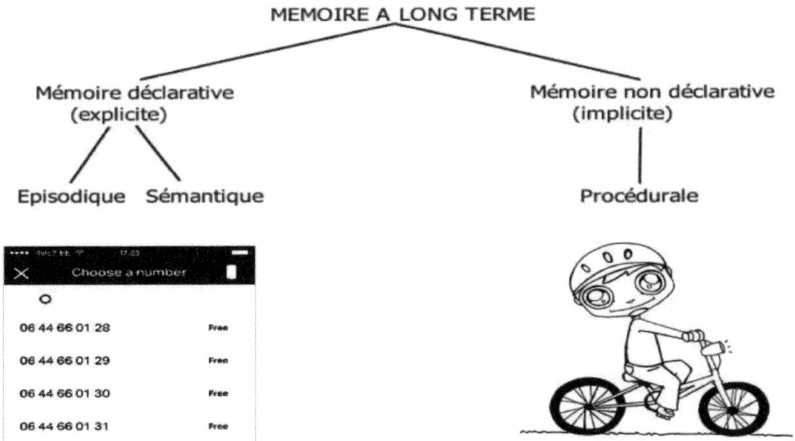

Figure A - Different types of memory. Image adapted from Squire [1992]

Understanding this type of knowledge, and acquiring and extracting it, has been and continues to be the subject of much research. In particular, there is a paradox in this implicit knowledge: it is both the most sought-after (linked to the individual, it carries more information than data [Malhotra, 2000; Crié, 2003], but it is also the least accessible.

But when it comes to sharing knowledge with others, especially expertise, know-how and experience in a particular field, it's implicit and explicit knowledge as a whole that needs to be shared.

In business, for example, the sharing and transmission of knowledge is a real strategic priority. Extracting expertise, i.e. specialized and advanced skills in a field, is all the more complex as there are several stages in the acquisition of these skills, according to which experts may or may not verbalize their knowledge [Hoffman, 2014].

In fact, our brains transform the knowledge we acquire as our skills increase. Do you drive today as you did when you first got your licence? Probably not!

What to remember?

There are two types of knowledge: explicit knowledge, which can be acquired through a conscious effort to learn it (definitions, new concepts, telephone numbers, rules of conduct, etc.) and implicit knowledge, which is learned without our knowledge, through repetition, imitation and experience. Both types of knowledge are important for an individual, as it is the combination of the two that shapes the individuals we are. Indeed, reading, understanding and learning all the Highway Code is no substitute for real driving experience, as it is through experience that we develop many of our reflexes. Yet it's the combination of the two that makes us good drivers.

If the means of acquiring explicit knowledge seem clear (reading, verbal transmission and rote learning), how do we acquire implicit knowledge? How does experience become implicit knowledge?

A description of the objects that make up the context of the A.I. system domain, in several forms:

- Description-classification :
"the canary is a bird".
- Description-structure :
"the windshield is a part of the bodywork of a car, truck or coach".
- Description-definition :
"a chair is a piece of furniture with 4 legs, 1 back and 1 seat".

Operational knowledge of the objects described above:

- Laws, theorems: "speed is given by the distance covered over the time taken to cover it".
- Rules of expertise: "if a bird is young, it's a canary".
- Strategies: "if golf then consult individual sports".

Knowledge representation in A.I. :

- **In the form of production rules (or propositional logic) : IF...THEN...**
if John is a man**, then** John is mortal.
- **Atlogic from first order or the calculation of predicates :**
Man(x) **then** mortal(x).
- **In the form of semantic networks :**

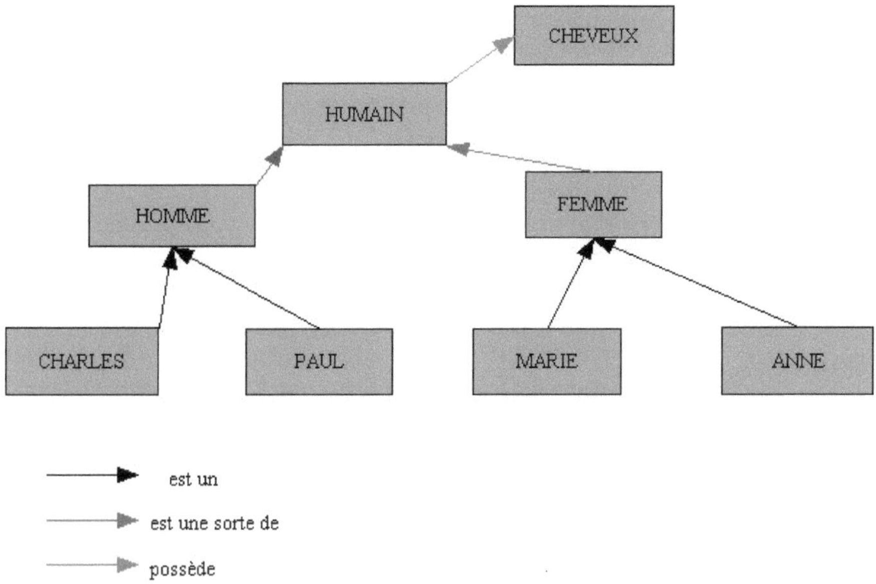

- **Atform object, frame, schemas** Most expert systems use a knowledge representation à rules from production rules **N.B.:** Some S.E. systems combine several formalisms. Knowledge

representation is linked to the subject matter.

- **Propositional or first-order logic** for the automatic demonstration of mathematical theorems.
- **Semantic networks** for natural language analysis and machine translation.
- **Production rules** for the description a circumscribed domain perfectly known by an expert.
- **etc...**

It is in the knowledge base that we will store the knowledge or know-how that will enable us, for example, to :

- playing chess,
- translate from French to English and vice-versa,
- recognize airplane and ship profiles...,
- solve mathematical problems.

The factual basis of the problem to be solved :

The fact base, also known as working memory, contains the initial hypotheses, i.e. the data specific to the problem to be solved.

- The mathematical assumptions of a problem to be solved.
- Elements that can help identify a disease.
- etc...

These assumptions can be formalized differently depending on the system.

Example 1.1:

SPHINX expert system.

FACTS: (40° fever, pimples, weight loss).

Example 1.2:

EXPERT expert system.

FACTS: (ANIMAL has feathers), (ANIMAL flies)

The fact base will be progressively enriched at the request of the expert system, so that it can progress towards the solution. For example, with the initial facts Example 2, the expert system finds the fact that ANIMAL is a bird. The fact base will contain: (ANIMAL has feathers), (ANIMAL flies), (ANIMAL is a bird).

This fact base can act as an auxiliary memory, storing all intermediate results. They can be used to keep track of the system's reasoning. They can explain the origin of the knowledge deduced by the expert system.

Facts, rules, reasoning:

We assume that reasoning is formalized in production rules. A rule takes the form :

IF Condition_1 and Condition_2 and Condition_3 ... and Condition_n **THEN** Action_1 and Action_2 and Action_3 ... and Action_p.

Example 1.3:
IF the animal lays eggs and the animal flies **THEN** the animal is a bird.

The left part is a premise. The right-hand side is a conclusion. Such a rule is also called an inference. The left-hand part expresses conditions. If all the conditions are satisfied, the other part becomes true.

Set of rules= **the rules base= the knowledge base,**
Set of facts= **the basis of facts.**

How does an expert system work in practice?

Example 1.4: ANIMALS expert system

ANIMALS" rule base:	ANIMALS" fact base:
• **R1** **IF** the animal is bird and the animal weighs less of 10 gr **THEN** the animal is a hummingbird. • **R2** **IF** the animal flies and the animal lays from eggs **THEN** the animal is a bird	• Animal flies • Animal weight less than 10 gr • Animal lays eggs

The operating mechanism or inference engine takes a rule and looks in the fact base to see if the stored facts will make the rule's premise true.

Let's take the first **R1** rule: one of the conditions is not met. We don't know if the animal is a bird. This fact is not in the fact base. The next rule **is R2**: the conditions are true. fact base contains the two conditions animal flies and animal lays eggs. The rule is executed. An additional fact is added to the fact base: "the animal is a bird".

New basis of facts "ANIMALS :
• Animal flies • Animal weight less than 10 gr • Animal lays eggs • Animal is bird

Now let's draw rule **R1** again: the conditions are true, the rule is executed. A new fact is added to the fact base: "the animal is a hummingbird".

Example 1.5: Expert system CITY

the "city" rule base:	based on "city" facts:
• **R1** **So** beautiful cityand very good restaurants **then** a city that despises travel. • **R2** **If** city historical **so** worth the trip. • **R3: If** welcoming natives and traditions **so** worth the trip. • **R4: If** monuments and abundant vegetation **so** beautiful city. • **R5** **If** tradition **so** good restaurants. • **R6** **If** restaurants 3 stars **so** very good restaurants. • **R7** **If** restaurants 3 toques **so** very good restaurants. • **R8: If** museums and old town **then** historic city. • **R9: If** Provence and seaside **then** welcoming natives.	• Green parks • Wide avenues • monuments • 3 toques restaurants • ancient city
• **R10** **If** parks green and avenues wide **then** abundant vegetation.	

Example 1.6: ABC expert system

Consider the following knowledge base:

Initial fact base :

{H,K}

Rule base :

- **R1 :** A --> E
- **R2 :** B --> D

- **R3 :** H --> A
- **R4:** E and G --> C
- **R5:** E and K --> B
- **R6:** D and E and K --> C
- **R7:** G and K and F --> A

The **R1** rule means IF A THEN E ("From A we can deduce E")

The theorem demonstrator proposes to induce new facts from the knowledge base and the ***modus ponens*** rule, i.e. the rule: **"If p is true and if p --> q then q is true"**.

Two general demonstration strategies are then possible:

Forward chaining: start from the initial fact base; trigger all rules whose premises are satisfied; add the facts thus obtained; continue until "saturation" is reached.

In the previous example, we obtain the following derivation chain:

- H --> A (R3) and the fact base B= {A,H,K}
- A --> E (R1) and B= {A,E,H,K}
- E and K --> B (R5) and B = {A,B,E,H,K}
- B --> D (R2) and B= {A,B,D,E,H,K}
- D and E and K --> C (R6) and B = {A,B,C,D,E,H,K}

Backward chaining: suppose we're trying to show whether fact D is true; that's the goal. We look at all the rules that have the goal in their consequences. Each of these rules is considered: if all its premises are satisfied in the initial fact base, the goal has been reached; otherwise, the unknown premises are recorded as new goals and the cycle is repeated for each of them.

In the previous example :

- Consider rule (R2) and define B as the new goal.
- We then consider rule (R5) and define E as the new goal (since K is in the fact base).
- Consider rules (R3) and (R7). (R3) allows us to conclude.

Example 1.7:

In the field of botany, let's consider the following **rule base**:

1. **If** flower **and** seed **then** phanerogram

2. **If** phanerogramin **and** bare seed **then** fir tree
3. **If** phanerogramin **and** 1-cotyledon **then** monocotyledon
4. **If** phanerogramin **and** 2-cotyledon **then** dicotyledon
5. **If** monocot **and** rhizome **then** thrush
6. **If** dicotyledonous**, then** anemone
7. **If** monocotyledonous **and not** rhizome**, then** lilac
8. **If** leaf **and** flower **then** cryptogam
9. **If** cryptogam **and not** root**, then** moss
10. **If** cryptogam **and** root **then** fern
11. **If not** leaves **and** plant **then** thallophyte
12. **If** thallophyte **and** chlorophyll **then** algae
13. **If** thallophyte **and not** chlorophyll **then** fungus
14. **If not** leaf **and not** flower **and not** plant **then** colibacillus

So, 1. means that "if the plant has a flower and a seed, then the plant is a phanerogramin". The problem is then to determine a plant with the following characteristics:
{rhizome, flower, seed, 1-cotyledon}.

This will be **the basis for the initial facts**.

In forward chaining, we obtain the following derivation chain:

- 1. --> phanerogram
- 3. --> monocotyledon
- 5. --> lily of the valley

Hence the **"lily of the valley"** solution, as the other rules don't kick in.

How to enrich and maintain the knowledge base :

Once the choice of representation has been made for a given knowledge base, it needs to be populated and then maintained: this is the role of the data acquisition module. The database must be easily manipulated and extensible to add, modify or delete stored knowledge, thanks to its representation symbolism.

Depending on the system, new knowledge is acquired through :

- Cognitive engineers.
- The expert.
- The system itself, thanks to its operating system...
- Machine learning.
- Automatic acquisition, for physical counters in particular.

Exercises :

Exercise 1:

From the "city" rule base and the associated fact base, we make the following deductions:

Initial fact base

- Green parks
- Wide avenues
- monuments
- restaurants 3 toques
- ancient city

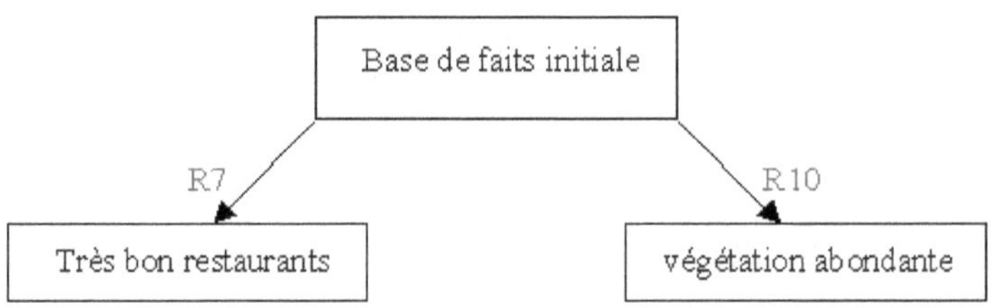

Initial fact base

- Green parks
- Wide avenues
- monuments
- restaurants 3 toques
- ancient city
- very good restaurants
- abundant vegetation

Complete the fact base by making the following deductions.

Exercise 2:

Using the "city" rule base and the associated fact base, we want to check whether the city is a city worth traveling to. Construct the solution in the form of a graph.

CHAPTER IV. ARTIFICIAL INTELLIGENCE PROGRAMMING

Computer languages are designed to describe all the information and consecutive actions a computer needs to execute. The language used by the processor is machine language, also known as binary language. However, machine language is not easily understood by humans, so an intermediate language (assembler) must be used, which is then transformed into machine language to be used by the processor. Assembly language was therefore the first computer language to be used. However, it is processor-dependent and not portable. Computer languages have several advantages:

They are easier to understand than machine language.

They allow for greater probability. Generally speaking, computer languages fall into three categories:

- ✓ Interpreted languages.
- ✓ Compiled languages.
- ✓ Intermediate languages.

Interpreted language

A program written in an interpreted language needs an auxiliary (interpreter) to translate the program's instructions as you go along, e.g. MathLab, SciLab, Prolog, which we're going to use as a case study, and so on.

Compiled language

A program written in a compiled language is translated once and for all by an auxiliary program (compiler) to generate a new, autonomous file.

The advantages of a compiled language are:

It's a stand-alone language, as it doesn't need a separate program to run. What's more, since the translation is done once and for all, it's faster to execute.

It guarantees source code security, e.g. Pascal, C, C++, Fortan, etc.

Intermediate language

These are languages that belong to the first two categories, e.g. Java, Python etc.

A program is a succession of instructions that can be executed by the computer.

In general, a program is a simple text file (written in a text editor), called a source file.

A source file contains program lines called source code. Once completed, the source file must be compiled (translated into executable code). Compilation takes place in two stages:

The compiler transforms the source code into object code (translating the file into machine language) and saves it in an object file.

The compiler then calls on a linker or binder, which integrates into the final file all the additional elements (functions or libraries) referred to in the program.

After link editing, an executable file is created, containing everything the program needs to run autonomously. The file thus created has an **.exe** extension (executable file).

IV.1. The 5 programming languages artificial intelligence

What programming languages are used by artificial intelligence professionals?

Here are the 5 most commonly used languages.

IV.1.1. Python

Python is every AI programmer's favorite, but have you ever wondered why it occupies a special place in AI and machine learning?

Well, it comes with a large number of built-in libraries. For some languages, you have to learn the language first. However, this is not the case with Python.

Python basics

For each AI project, you can choose the libraries best suited to your project (SciPy, NumPy, Pybrain, etc.).

There is a large open source community

Since Python involves a large number of algorithms, it makes it easy to test and write simple code.

Python is platform agnostic

IV.1.2. R language

R is a popular programming language for statistical analysis, i.e. Big Data. It used to be the programming language of choice for data analysts. However, R has had a considerable impact on AI in recent years, as data science and AI have converged.

R basics

It is perfectly suited to AI modeling. For visualization purposes, R is the most powerful. R has a huge community and supporters

Some of the world's biggest companies, such as Google, use R for data modeling, visualization and analysis.

IV.1.3. Java language

Java is considered one of the best languages for AI projects. Java basics

For example, if we take AI programming in Java, it is generally used to create models for machine learning, genetic programming, multi-robot systems and so on.

The fact that Java is object-oriented and highly scalable is a perfect match for large-scale projects.

IV.1.4. Prolog language

They say you can boost the performance of your chatbots by using Prolog. This is a logic programming language specifically used to perform natural language processing. Ever heard of Eliza? It's one of the chatbots that were written, and that's how Prolog came into being.

Prolog essentials Highlights:

- ✓ Automatic back-tracking,
- ✓ Pattern matching
- ✓ Data structuring.

IV.1.5. Lisp language

Used by engineers looking to broaden their horizons in the field of AI, Lisp is a much less widespread language.

Invented by John McCarthy (the father of AI in 1958), Lisp is considered one of the oldest languages used for AI development.

Lisp basics

Excellent prototyping capabilities Automatic waste collection

Dynamic creation newer objects

The development cycle provides for interactive evaluation of expressions and recompilation of functions even when the program is still running. With the progress made in recent years, many Lisp functions have been migrated to other languages, which has affected Lisp's uniqueness.

IV.2. How do algorithms become intelligent?

As algorithms play an ever-increasing role in our daily lives, the question of endowing them with a conscience is emerging in the debate. How are these artificial intelligences inspired by humans? How does AI work today, and where is it heading? But above all: how does this mirror effect benefit humans? These are just some of the questions to which scientists from all walks of life have contributed answers.

Aldous Huxley[6] said that "*there are three kinds of intelligence: human intelligence, animal intelligence and military intelligence*". Isn't one of them missing? In 1956, at the Dartmouth conference, the term
The term "*artificial intelligence*" was used for the first time. "*[The conference]*

[6] A great British novelist and philosopher

created a new discipline and indicated a few avenues, such as neural networks, machine learning and the study of creativity, on which research then focused," details Jean-Gabriel Ganascia, artificial intelligence researcher and chairman of the CNRS ethics committee, in an interview with Les Echos.

Since then, researchers have been working to inject notions of human intelligence into machines. But what exactly is human intelligence? It is located in the brain, and is associated with the mental and cognitive capacities required to solve a problem, or to adapt to one's environment. Emotional, practical, economic... intelligence has many facets, making its definition complex and controversial. It varies according to the times, the thinkers and the discoveries made about how it works - which remains highly mysterious, even today.

IV.2.1. To think or to imitate, that is the question

As early as 1950, Alan Turing, whose work laid the scientific foundations of computer science, refocused the debate artificial intelligence with the famous "Turing test", in his book *Computing Machinery and Intelligence*. He suggests replacing the question "*Can machines think*?
"Can machines imitate human intelligence? To measure this, Turing proposed testing the ability of machines to imitate human conversation through written questions and answers. If the human interlocutor is unable to discern whether he or she is speaking to a computer or another human, the software has passed the test.

In other words, AI software today passes the Turing test with flying colors. Since 1994, no human has managed to beat the Canadian Chinook program at English checkers, and Libratus earned $1.76 million plucking professional poker players in 2017. These advances are not limited to gaming. In 2012, Google's AI was able to recognize a cat after watching YouTube videos. In 2016, IBM's Watson program diagnosed rare leukemia in a Japanese patient in just ten minutes. How did algorithms become so *smart*?

IV.2.2. Algorithms on the way to school

Artificial intelligence programming has evolved with advances in computer science and discoveries in neuroscience. *Deep learning* is the most promising *machine learning* technology. It uses an architecture of interconnected artificial neurons, inspired by that of the brain. This network is capable processing large quantities information and learning progressively from images, text or data.

These *deep learning* capabilities continue to be developed, with a recent paradigm shift opening up exciting prospects.

Rather than continuing to program software to perform tasks according to predefined scenarios, algorithms are now asked to find the rule themselves, based example. Just like babies discovering the world: bombarded with information about their environment, they gradually deduce rules which they apply without even being aware of their existence. This change in approach now makes it possible to train AIs to carry out a wide variety of tasks, and to envisage an almost infinite progression in their capabilities.

IV.2.3. Is science without conscience the ruin of soul?

For the moment, the progress made by algorithms responds to very specific situations: diagnosing an illness, driving a car, recommending a choice of reading material or itinerary, and so on. Tomorrow's challenge is to create an artificial intelligence capable of linking all these uses, which presupposes communication and understanding between AIs.

This idea of a super AI raises the question of its consciousness. Serge Tisseron, PhD in psychology and author of *Le jour où mon robot m'aimera. Vers l'empathie artificielle*, offers this definition in a BNP Paribas workshop:
"*Self-awareness enables man to perceive himself as the subject of a story, with a past and projects. We can imagine that the complexification of artificial neural networks could produce a form of self-awareness. But such machines would have a fundamentally different experience of the world and of themselves than we do, and no one knows what it would consist of*". This consciousness would give them the possibility of elaborating their own project of existence, even if, as Serge Tisseron reminds us, we're still a long way from that today!

The next step in the evolution of AI could be to endow algorithms with an artificial personality, enabling them simulate emotions. These reactions would remain totally artificial, and incomparable with the consciousness of living beings. Robots could, however, acquire decision-making autonomy, while continuing to evolve within a human-defined framework.

IV.2.4. From the trainer's point of view

This flexibility of artificial intelligence is highly beneficial when put to use in the service of learning... human learning, this time! Integrating algorithms into the learning process enables us to adapt to the level of knowledge, the memorization method, the pace of acquisition of each learner, and above all to the functioning of the human brain. The algorithms used in Memory Anchoring® optimize the long-term memorization of new knowledge, using "*spaced learning*" for example, a repetition technique that promotes long-term recall.

IV.3. Algorithms: what are they and what do they do?

In the age of Big Data, Machine Learning and artificial intelligence, algorithms have become ubiquitous in our lives. But what exactly is an algorithm? Discover the definition of the term, its use cases and some examples of the most famous and massively used algo's.

The term algorithm **was coined by the mathematician Mohammed Ibn Musa- Al Khwarizmi,** in the course of the ninth century . With the rise of artificial intelligence, the term is increasingly used and has joined the category of "buzzwords".

Today, algorithms are used to find love, to invest in the best stocks, to predict crime, to organize web search results and for millions of other applications. Algorithms are ubiquitous, driving our economy, our society and perhaps even the way we think. **But what actually is an algorithm?**

IV.3.1. What is an algorithm?

In the field of mathematics, where the term originated, an algorithm can be seen as **an ordered and finite set of operations that must be followed in order to solve a problem**. As a simple example, let's take a recipe. In each recipe, a specific procedure must be followed in order. The different steps in the recipe represent the operations that make up the algorithm.

Where things get a little more complicated is that the purpose of an algorithm is to solve a problem and therefore produce a result. If we want to create an algorithm that can function in the real world, we need to include instructions that enable it to adapt to the different situations it may encounter. This is why **algorithms are like gigantic "trees" of instructions**.

IV.3.2. The history of algorithms

By the way, why are algorithms called "algorithms"? The story begins in the 9th century, with **the astronomer and mathematician Muhammad ibn Mūsa al-**

Khwarizmī.

This Persian scholar made great discoveries in science, mathematics and the numbering system we still use today. His name is **the Persian word for the region where he was born: Khwãrezm**.

Over the centuries, its reputation has grown worldwide. Outside the Middle East, **his name was distorted to become "Algoritmi"**. This version of his name was later adapted as an English term for the step-by-step recipes we refer to as "algorithms".

IV.3.3. What is a computer algorithm?

To perform any task, a computer needs a computer program. To work, a computer program must **tell the computer** exactly what to do, step by step.

The **computer then "executes" the program**, mechanically following each step to reach the goal. But the computer also needs to be told "how" to do what it needs to do. This is the role of the computer algorithm.

Computer algorithms work by means of **input and output**. They receive input, and apply each step of the algorithm to this information to generate an output.

For example, **a search engine** is an algorithm that receives a search as input. It searches its database for items corresponding to the words in the query, and then produces the results.

Computers don't understand human language, so a computer algorithm has to be **translated into code** written in a programming language. There are many different languages, such as Logo, Scrach, Python, R... each with its own specificities and best suited to a specific use case.

IV.3.4. What are algorithms good for?

Algorithms have countless use cases. In the field of technology and computing, when a developer creates a program, he is in fact creating a set of algorithms. Indeed, **a computer program is a set of commands given to the machine**, written in a specific language, in order to perform a series of specific operations to obtain a result.

Since a computer is (still) incapable of understanding human language, **the programmer uses a programming language**. This language acts as a bridge between human language and the language the machine can understand. Thanks to this tool, the programmer can create a series of instructions that the computer can "understand".

Algorithms: some well-known examples

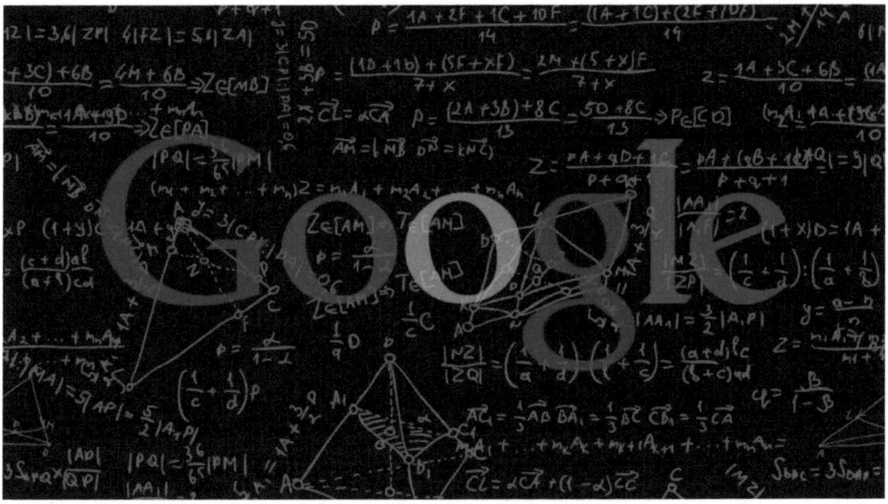

To help you better understand what an algorithm is, let's take a look **at some very famous examples**, commonly used by much of humanity.

First and foremost is **Google's PageRank**. This is a set of algorithms used by Google to determine the importance of documents indexed by its web search engine. So, when you perform a search on Google, it's one of the elements that determine the order in which results are displayed. PageRank is without doubt the most widely used algorithm in the world.

Another example is **Facebook's Timeline**. The content that Facebook displays on your News Feed is chosen by a set of algorithms. These decide what content to display based on various parameters such as your personal tastes, your reactions to previously proposed content and much more.

Another example is **high-frequency trading algorithms**. These are the algorithms used by the world's leading financial institutions, enabling them to place orders on the market according to the profit they hope to make and the market conditions at a given moment. Today, these algorithms have more influence on the global economy than human traders, and are responsible for the circulation of billions of dollars every day.

A final example is **the Round Robin algorithm**. This is an algorithm widely used in computing, since it enables computers to determine which tasks they should perform first. As a general rule, this algo determines how much time the processor will spend on each task in progress.

IV.3.5. Algorithms and Machine Learning

Machine Learning algorithms are a specific category of algorithms. Rather than receiving specific instructions on the task to be performed, they are **able to "learn" from data**.

Today, they are used on a massive scale to create **recommendation engines, make predictions or analyze data**. Based on the data provided as examples, Machine Learning algorithms can make better decisions.

Today, these algorithms **are omnipresent on the Internet**. They determine what you see on your Facebook news feed, the ads that appear in your Gmail inbox, or the movies and series that Netflix recommends.

There is **a wide variety of algorithms** used for Machine Learning. They can be grouped into several distinct categories.

In the case of **supervised learning** algorithms, the input data is called training data, and is labeled beforehand by humans to tell the machine what it corresponds to.

The model is trained on this data, and must be **able to make accurate predictions**. The training process continues until the desired level of accuracy is achieved. Examples include

logistic regression algorithms and the back propagation neural network.

In case of **unsupervised learning**, the input data is unlabeled and has no known outcome. The model itself must observe structures and trends in the data. This may involve, for example, reducing redundancy via a mathematical process, or organizing data by similarity.

This type of learning is used to clustering, dimensionality reduction or association rule learning problems. Examples include **the Apriori and K-means algorithms**.

Finally, in case of **semi-supervised learning**, the input data is a mixture of labeled and unlabeled examples. The problem to be solved is indicated, but the model must organize the data itself to make predictions. This type of learning is used for classification and regression.

Algorithms can also be grouped **by similarity of operation**. Broad categories include regression algorithms, regularization algorithms, decision treesBayesian algorithms and clustering algorithms.

There are also association rule learning algorithms, artificial neural network algorithms, learning algorithms and dimension reduction algorithms.

These families of algorithms are among the most widely used in Machine Learning. However, there are many others, and some algorithms belong to **several categories at once**.

IV.3.6. Data encryption algorithms

Algorithms are used to encrypt data or communication lines. This **protects data in the event of theft** or intrusion on the system on which it is stored.

To achieve this, mathematical algorithms are used. The algorithm receives the data as input, and **converts it into another format** as output. Once encrypted, the data may resemble a text composed of random symbols, or even an image unrelated to the original content.

IV.3.7. Algorithms and automation

Another use case for algorithms **is automation software**. These programs work by following rules to complete tasks. They are therefore made up of multiple algorithms.

For example, such software can extract all billing information received via email and transfer it to a spreadsheet. To accomplish this task, it is necessary to set up **a series of rules and conditions to be followed: an algorithm**.

In this example, each email received acts as an input. The emails are then processed in **a step-by-step process** to complete the task.

The process might involve scanning each email for key terms. Messages containing these terms **are then passed on to the next stage, and so on,** in order to identify and extract the most relevant data. The output is the information placed in a spreadsheet at the end of the process.

Another example: **many sports bettors** create automation algorithms. Here's an example from the TipStreet YouTube channel, which even explains how to create your own algo.

IV.3.8. Limits and dangers of algorithms

Algorithms offer many possibilities, but they remain simple sets of instructions. They **are created by humans**, and can therefore be flawed.

programmers computers spend a lot of their time **correcting errors in algorithms**. Because of a simple mistake, an algorithm can produce inaccurate results. Unfortunately, these errors are not always identified in time.

Beyond errors, **algorithms can be biased** by the perception or even the will of the humans who create them. Take the example of an algorithm designed for recruitment. If the person creating it considers (wrongly) that a white man is systematically a better candidate than a woman of color, the algorithm will be based on this perception and will therefore be biased.

This problem of bias is **even more dangerous** for artificial intelligence algorithms. These algorithms feed on the data they are provided with, and can therefore perpetuate the misperceptions and biases of the past.

For example, knowing that most high-tech companies **lack ethnic diversity**, a Machine Learning algorithm will be able to deduce from past data that diverse candidates are profiles to be avoided.

This is a real problem right now, as biased algorithms **perpetuate discrimination**. Facial recognition systems associate people of color with criminals, and chatbots become quickly racist. Several companies are therefore looking for solutions to remove bias from AI algorithms...

IV.3.9. How do you design ethical algorithms?

avoid the abuses associated with algorithms and AI, it is important **adopt good ethical practices right from the design stage**. To achieve this, we need to focus on several key points.

First of all, we need to **ask ourselves what the algorithm will be used for**. The application itself must be ethical. Algorithms and AI systems are sometimes misused by third parties.

Many Machine Learning scientists and developers are now **protesting the immoral use of their algorithms**. For example, Microsoft employees have protested against the use of HoloLens augmented reality by the US military, while Google teams have raised their voices against the development of automated weapons.

It is also very important to ensure **that the algorithm's training data is not biased**. The data itself must be ethical for the algorithm to be ethical.

Many Machine Learning algorithms used today in commercial products are **heavily biased to cause data** exploited for their training. For example, Amazon decided to stop relying on AI for recruitment, as its system was highly discriminatory.

While the company had tried to remove gender indicators from the system to avoid bias, the algorithm was still able to detect them. So, data and Machine Learning **often reflect and magnify our own unconscious biases**. It's essential to take this into account.

In addition to the data, **the "weights" assigned to the various algorithm functions** must also be taken into account. When optimizing weightings, it's important to take ethics into account.

Finally, **the data features and characteristics analyzed by AI** must enable an ethical result. They must offer an accurate representation, to avoid unpleasant surprises later on.

Generally speaking, a key point for ethics is **diversity within developer teams**. Lack of diversity is a major contributor to dataset bias, just as it has led to clumsy advertising campaigns in the marketing field.

What does the future hold for algorithms?

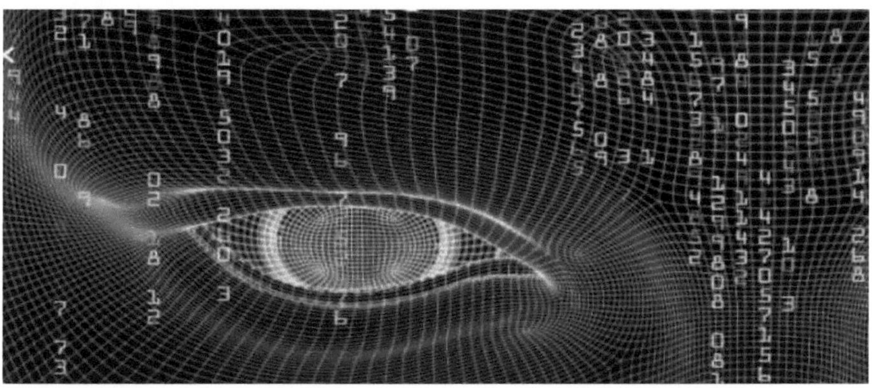

It's hard to predict the future of algorithms. On the other hand, it seems certain that **the future belongs to algorithms**.

Indeed, algorithms are at the heart of revolutionary emerging technologies such as artificial intelligence, machine learning, autonomous vehicles and virtual assistants. In the years to come, we can expect **new algorithm-based technologies** to **emerge**...

CHAPTER V. EXPERT SYSTEM DESIGN (PROLOG CASE STUDY)

This chapter deals with the practical use of Prolog for interactive logic programs, starting from problems and facts that the students have already mastered.

BIBLIOGRAPHICAL REFERENCES

1. **BONNET Alain, HATON Jean-Paul, TRUONG Jean- Michel** , *Système experts : vers la maîtrise technique*, InterÉditions, 1986.
2. **CARDON Alain,** *Modeling and design a machine Approche de la conscience artificielle*, Vuibert, 2004.
3. **TURING Alan, GIRARD Jean-Yves**, The machine from Machine, Computers and Intelligence, 1995, pp. 133-174.
4. **C.FLAMENT**, *Graph theory and social structures*, Ed. Mouton, Paris, 1968, 166 pages.
5. **VIGNAUX Georges,** *Les sciences cognitives : une introduction*, Biblio Essais, Paris, 1994.
6. **J.-L. LAURIERE,** *Eléments de programmation dynamique*, Collection Programmation, Ed. Gauthier-Villars, Paris, 1979.
7. **CHALLONER Jack,** *L'Intelligence artificielle : Un guide d'initiation au futur de l'informatique et de la robotique,* Pearson Education, 2003.
8. **LAURIERE Jean-Louis,** *Intelligence Artificielle,* Eyrolles, 1986.
9. **ALLIOT Jean-Marc and SCHIEX Thomas**, *Intelligence artificielle et informatique théorique,* CEPADUES, 2002.
10. **DELAHAYE Jean-Paul**, *Logical tools for artificial intelligence,* Eyrolles, 1987.
11. **Michel LE SEAC'H**, *développer un système expert,* published by éditests, 1989.
12. **CLAIRE Rémy**, *L'Intelligence artificielle,* 1994.
13. **RUSSELL STUART Jonathan and NORVIG Peter**, *Artificial Intelligence,* Pearson Education, 2006.
14. **Chraibi Kaadoud, Ikram and Delmas, Alexandra.** 2018, *Cognition or what is cognitive science?* Published on the https://scilogs.fr/intelligence-mecanique blog,
URL: https://scilogs.fr/intelligence-mecanique/la-cognition-ou-quest-ce- que-les-sciences-cognitives/
15. **Crié, Dominique,** 2003, *De l'extraction des connaissances au knowledge management.* Revue française de gestion, (5) :59-79.
16. **Dienes, Zoltan and Berry, Dianne,** 1997, *Implicit learning: Below the subjective threshold.* Psychonomic bulletin & review, 4(1) :3-23.

2\. **Dienes, Zoltan, Broadbent, Donald and Berry, Dianne C,** 1991. *Implicit and explicit knowledge bases in artificial grammar learning.* Journal of

Experimental Psychology : Learning, Memory, and Cognition, 17(5) :875.

3. **Dubuc, Bruno**, 2002. Memory and learning. URL : http://lecerveau.mcgill.ca/flash/i/i_07/i_07_p/i_07_p_tra/i_07_p_tra.htm l

4. **Hoffman, Robert R,** 2014. *The psychology of expertise: Cognitive research and empirical AI.* Psychology Press.

5. **Malhotra, Yogesh,** 2000. *Knowledge management and new organization forms: A framework for business model innovation.* Knowledge management and virtual organizations, 2(1) :13-27.

6. **Nonaka, Ikujiro and Takeuchi, Hirotaka,** 1995. *The knowledge-creating company: How Japanese companies create the dynamics of innovation.* Oxford university press.

7. **Schacter, Daniel L,** 1987. *Implicit memory: History and current status. Journal of experimental psychology*: learning, memory, and cognition, 13(3) :501.

8. **Smith, Elizabeth A**, 2001. *The role of tacit and explicit knowledge in the workplace.* Journal of knowledge Management, 5(4) :311-321.

9. **Squire, Larry R,** 1992. *Declarative and nondeclarative memory: Multiple brain systems supporting learning and memory.* Journal of cognitive neuroscience, 4(3) :232-243.

10. **Squire, Larry R and Zola, Stuart M**, 1996. *Structure and function of declarative and nondeclarative memory systems.* Proceedings of the National Academy of Sciences, 93(24) :13515-13522.

MIX
Papier aus verantwortungsvollen Quellen
Paper from responsible sources
FSC® C105338

Printed by Books on Demand GmbH, Norderstedt / Germany